NATURE MEDITATIONS

Nature Meditations

Hazrat Inayat Khan

Omega Publications, Inc.
New Lebanon, NY

Manufactured in the United States of America.

Published by Omega Publications, Inc.
256 Darrow Road, New Lebanon, NY 12125
www.omegapub.com

Cover photo: *Veils of Orographic Lifting* by Brian Post, used by permission of Mount Washington Observatory.

Interior art work by Kamila Mirabai Chrin.

Cover and interior design by Karim White.
Typeset in InDesign CS using Adobe Caslon Pro.

Managing editor and production supervisor Vajra Dana Densmore. Textual research by Sharif Graham. Proofreading and editorial assistance by Tajmina Aviva. Production support provided by Green Lion Press.

Printed and bound by McNaughton-Gunn, Saline, Michigan.

Cataloging in Publication Data
Inayat Khan
Nature Meditations
1. Nature. 2. Spirituality. 3. Mysticism. 4. Sufism.
I. Khan, Inayat (1882–1927) II. Title

Library of Congress Control Number: 2004113500
ISBN 0-930872-72-X

CONTENTS

General 59

Addendum 77

Inayat Khan Biographical Note 91

PREFACE TO THE 2005 EDITION

Hazrat Inayat Khan dictated the *Nature Meditations* to his secretary, Sheikh Sirdar van Tuyll, at his first Summer School in Wissous, France, in 1921.

Fikar is the practice of reciting a word or phrase silently on the breath as one inhales and exhales. The *Nature Meditations* are specifically designed for that purpose. The phrases were given so that they could be repeated silently on the breath as a form of spiritual practice. This is indicated in the text by roman type for the inhalation, parentheses where the breath is held, and italics for the exhalation.

But what is the purpose of this? It is the use of the breath as a spiritual practice, enabling the words or phrases to penetrate into one's very being.

Pir-O-Murshid Inayat Khan on Breath

Fikar

The breath is like a swing which has a constant motion, and whatever is put in the swing, swings also with the movement of the breath. *Fikar*, therefore, is not a breathing practice. In *fikar* it is not necessary that one should breathe in a certain way, different from one's usual breathing. *Fikar* is to become conscious of the natural movement of the breath, and picturing breath as a swing, to put in that swing a certain thought, as a babe in the cradle, to rock it. Only the difference is rocking is an intentional activity on the part of the person who rocks the cradle. In *fikar* no effort must be made to change the rhythm of the breath; the breath must be left to its own usual rhythm. One need not try even to regulate the rhythm of the breath, for the whole mechanism of one's body is already working rhythmically. So the breath is rhythmical by nature and it is the very breath itself which cause man to distinguish rhythm.

What is important in *fikar* is not the rhythm but the concentration. *Fikar* is swinging the concentrated thought with the movement of breath, for breath is life and it gives life to the thought which is repeated with the breath. On the rhythm of the breath the circulation of the blood and the pulsation of the heart and head depend, which means that the whole mechanism of the body, also of the mind, is directed by the rhythm of the breath. When a thought is attached to the breath by concentration, then the effect of that thought reaches every atom of one's mind and body. Plainly speaking, the thought held in *fikar* runs with the circulation of the blood through every vein and tube of the body, and the influence of that thought is spread through every faculty of the mind. Therefore the reaction of the *fikar* is the resonance of the same thought expressing itself through one's thought, speech and action. So in time the thought one holds in *fikar* becomes the reality of one's self. So he who contemplates on God in time arrives at a state where his self turns into the being of God. (From *The Gathas, Pasi Anfas: Breath: Gatha II*, p. 147.)

INTRODUCTION

by
Pir Vilayat Inayat Khan

Disciples of Hazrat Inayat Khan who had the great privilege of attending the Summer School at Suresnes in the suburbs of Paris, and especially the earlier one in the midst of the wheat fields at Wissous, will never forget the impression of perfect resonance between the master and nature. While ostensibly breathing in the magnetism of the earth at each step, he was bestowing upon her his particular quality of cosmic power and opening his body to serve as a bridge conducting celestial magnetism into the bowels of the earth. Quickening the trees and flowers with a different life, his breath sanctified the whole union with the divine consciousness.

What solitude in nature meant to him comes across strongly in the last scenes of his play *The Bogey Man*. Here he portrays his real self, the recluse, in his natural setting, and hints at what an estrangement it meant to commune with worldly values made by man. Was not his nature to show how one can and should enrich and complete our secular way of life and adumbrate the values motivating the holy man, whose way of thinking he was representing?

In *Nature Meditations* Hazrat Inayat Khan gives us a means of introducing this way of thinking, feeling, and experiencing into our everyday routine. Obviously man's need for oneness with nature is not fulfilled simply by hiking or camping in nature, but by penetrating into the consciousness of the trees and the flowers, of the planet and the atoms, experiencing what it would be like to be that flower or tree and getting into the spirit of the wind on a landscape or of a musical note: in fact, switching to a totally different focus of consciousness, tuning in to a transfigured world which, as the Sufis say, "transpires through that which appears." This means discovering a whole other dimension of life and re-establishing a bond with nature that has been so often violated; and it requires a sacred tryst between man and nature, his promise to respect her and to sanctify his relationship with her in the name of God.

NATURE MEDITATIONS

Nature

by
Hazrat Inayat Khan

Anyone who has some knowledge of mysticism and of the lives of the mystics knows that what always attracts the mystic most is nature. Nature is his bread and wine; nature is his soul's nourishment; nature inspires him, uplifts him, and gives him the solitude for which his soul continually longs. Every soul born with a mystical tendency is constantly drawn towards nature, for in nature that soul finds its life's demand.

As it is said in the *Vadan**, "Art is dear to my heart, but nature is near to my soul."

Upon those who are without any tendency towards mysticism nature has a calming effect; to them it means a peaceful atmosphere. But to the mystic nature is everything. No wonder that the mystics, sages, and prophets of all ages sought refuge in nature from all the disturbing influences of daily life. They considered the caves of the mountains to be better than palaces; they enjoyed the shelter under a tree more than beautiful houses; they liked looking at the running water better than watching the passing crowds; they preferred the seashores to the great cities; they enjoyed watching the rising and the falling of the waves more than all the show that the world can produce; they loved to look at the moon, at the planets, at the stars in the sky more than at all the beautiful things made by man.

To a mystic the word nature has a wider meaning. According to the mystical point of view nature has four different aspects. The forest, the desert, hills and dales, mountains and rivers, sunrise and sunset, the moonlit

---

*Vadan is one of five short books of aphorisms, meditations, poems and prayers collected in *Complete Sayings of Hazrat Inayat Khan* and published by Omega Publications.

4

night, and the shining stars are one aspect of nature. Before a mystic they stand like letters, characters, figures made by the Creator to read if one is able to read them. The *sura* of the Qur'an which contains the first revelation of the Prophet includes the verse, "Read in the name of your Lord . . . who taught with the pen." The mystic, therefore, recognizes this manifestation as a written book; he tries to read these characters and enjoys what they reveal to him. To the mystic it is not only the waxing and waning of the moon, it has some other significance for him; it is not only the rising and the setting of the sun, it tells him something else; it is not only the positions of the stars, but their action and their influence relate something to the heart of the mystic. The mountains standing so silently, the patient trees of long tradition, the barren desert, the thick forest, not only have a calming effect upon the mystic, but they express something to him. The fluttering of the leaves comes to his ears as a whisper, the murmer of the winds falls on his ears as music, and the sound of little streams of water running in the forest, making their way through rocks and pebbles, is a symphony to the ears of the mystic. No music can be greater and higher and better than this. The crashing of the thunder, the soughing of the wind, the blowing of the morning breeze, all these convey to a mystic a certain meaning which is hidden behind them. For a mystic they make a picture of life, not a dead picture but a living picture which at every moment continually reveals a new secret, a new mystery to his heart.

And then we come to the next aspect of nature, an aspect which manifests through the lower creation. The silent little creatures crawling on the earth, the birds singing in the trees, the lion with its wrath, the elephant with its grandeur, the horse with its grace, and the deer with its beauty: all these tell the mystic something. He begins to see the meaning of the wrath of the lion and of the modesty of the deer; he listens to the words that come to his ears through the singing of the birds, for to him it is not a wordless song. The ancient mystics in their symbology used the head of the tiger, the form of the lion, the image of the eagle, and also pictures of the snake and the cow. They pictured them as a character which they had read through observing this aspect of nature.

There is an aspect of nature which is still more interesting, and to see it the mystic need not go away, for he sees it in the midst of the world. What is it? It is to read human nature and to watch its continual change, its progress, its degradation, its improvement. It is so interesting that in spite of all the difficulties that the world presents, one feels life worth living when one begins to notice how those who were going forward begin to go backward, and how those who were going backward begin to go forward; when one observes how a person, without sinking in the water, is drowned in life, and how a person who was drowning begins to swim and is saved; when one sees how from the top a person comes down to the bottom in a moment, and how a person who was creeping on the ground has at last arrived at the top; when one sees how friends turn into bitter enemies, and how bitter enemies one day become friends. To one who observes human nature keenly, it gives such an interest in life that he becomes sufficiently strong to bear all, to endure all, to stand all things patiently. One may observe this moving picture all through life, and it is never enough; one never tires of it.

And the fourth aspect of nature is seeing the divine nature, realizing the meaning of the saying that man proposes and God disposes. When one is able to see the works of God in life, another world is opened before one. Then a man does not look at the world as everybody else does, for he begins to see not only the machine going on but the engineer standing by its side, making the machine work. This offers a still greater interest, the greatest interest in life. If one were to be flayed or crucified one would not mind, for one rises above all pain and suffering, and one feels it worthwhile to be living and looking at this phenomenon that gives one in one's lifetime the proof of the existence of God.

It is these four aspects of life that are called *nature* by the mystics; to a Sufi they are his holy scripture. All the other sacred books of the world, however highly esteemed by the followers of the different religions, are interpretations of this book, given by those who were granted clear vision and who tried their best to give all they had learnt from it to humanity in our human language, which is a language of limitations.

Nature does not teach the glory of God; it need not teach this, as nature itself is the glory of God. People wish to study astrology and other subjects in order to understand better. But if we study astrology then we are sure to arrive at an interpretation which is given by a man; whereas what we should read from nature is what nature gives us, not what any book teaches us.

There comes a time, with the maturity of the soul, when every thing and every being begins to reveal its nature to us. We do not need to read people's lives; we do not need to read their theories. We know then that this wide nature in its four aspects is ever-revealing and that one can always communicate with it, but that in spite of this it is not the privilege of every soul to read it. Many souls remain blind with open eyes. They are in heaven, but not allowed to look at heaven; they are in paradise, but not allowed to enjoy the beauties of paradise. It is just like a person sleeping on a pile of gems and jewels. From the moment man's eyes open and he begins to read the book of nature he begins to live; and he continues to live forever.

Earth

I bend towards the mother earth
in delight of the father in heaven.

Trees

Let my mind bear sweet fruit and fragrant flowers,
as this tree is planted on the soil of thy spirit.

WITH BRANCHES DOWNWARDS:

I see thy hand
blessing me.

RISING UPWARDS:

Praying for me
with hands raised upwards.

IN THE NIGHT:

My heart stands in waiting and hope
as the trees stand still through the darkness of night.

Flowers

I see thy mystery
hidden under the petals of the flowers.

Flowers are
thy dancing rhythm.

In flowers I see
the female beauty of thy spirit.

The flowers tell me
how beautiful thou art.

In the color of flowers
I see the color of thy countenance.

In the form of flowers
I behold thy image.

I see thy skill, O perfect artist,
in the making of flowers.

Flowers speak to me
of thy loveliness.

Out of flowers comes a fragrance,
which moves my heart to ecstasy.

The sweet fragrance of the flowers
brings to me the message of thy sweetness.

Who made the flowers so beautiful,
(colored them and gave them fragrance),
it is thee, my Lord.

On Roses

The rose offers to me thy message of love;
I offer to thee my devotion in rose.

In the rose I see
thy delightful countenance.

Let my heart bloom in thy love
as the rose.

My lips are closed, with prayer in them,
as the rosebud.

Empower my heart that I may pull myself together
like the heart of the rose controlling its petals.

Let me retain thy beauty,
which I have as the rose.

The divine spark in me is as a drop from thy ocean;
let me preserve it as the rose preserves the dewdrop.

In the red rose I see
thy heart bleeding over the corruption of humanity.

In the white rose I see
the purity of thy divine being.

In the pink rose I see
thy divine love and compassion.

In the cream rose I see
thy wisdom.

In the yellow rose I see
thy divine light.

Oh, turn my heart red
like thy lovely red rose.

My heart turns into a pink rose
in thy divine love.

Landscape

I feel thy presence in this landscape
which draws my heart so close to thee.

This landscape in my heart
is a reflection of thy beauty.

Mountains

Let me stand by truth in all calamities
as the mountain stands unshaken through storms.

Strengthen my heart in thy faith
as the rock of the mountains.

Help me to climb the mountain path
which leads to thy shrine.

I look up to thee with raised head and hands
stretched
in worship as the mountains.

Let thy might be my might
to lift the mountains of life's responsibility.

For the Beauty of Spring, Fields with Flowers

I see the beloved's beauty
in all colors and forms.

Let my spirit reflect, O beloved,
the beauty of thy color and form.

For All That Gives Seed and Fruit

Thou art the life
and thou art life's sustenance.

Water

Let the stream of thy wisdom and joy rise in my soul
as the spring of water.

Open my heart
that thy stream may rise up as the spring.

Let my life become the spring of thy infinite life,
running eternally forever and ever.

Running water:

My life is running towards thee my ocean,
as the river runs to the sea.

Still water:

Let my heart reflect thy calm
as the stillness of the water.

Rain

Send the shower of thy mercy and compassion
on humanity.

Snow

Let thy knowledge cover my heart
as the snow covers the ground.

Let my heart melt in thy light
as the snow before the sun.

Let my heart show the purity of snow
in the path of righteousness.

Pour on me thy eternal life
as snow on earth.

Make my heart delighted
by the snowfall of thy knowledge of truth.

Ocean

Let my heart become the ocean
of thy divine perfection.

My head bends in humility and rises with thy might
as the ever-rising waves of the sea.

The waves of joy rise in my heart
when I see thy nature manifest in the sea.

I stand like the bubble
in thee, my ocean.

My life is a wave
of the ocean of thy eternal life.

Thou art the ocean
and I am the wave.

Let me not be drowned
in the sea of mortal life.

Teach me, Lord, to walk
over life's sea.

Clouds

STILL CLOUDS FILLED WITH COLOR AND LIGHT:

Let me reflect thy light through my thoughts
as the clouds reflect in color the light of the sun.

Let from my heart rise clouds
bringing to view thy beauty and color.

Let thy beauty shine through my heart
as through the clouds come, and spread out, the rays of the sun.

RAIN CLOUDS AND CLOUDS OF STORM:

While the clouds of thy mercy are to be sent on earth,
the feelings of my heart ascend towards thee.

When dark clouds surround the sky and people seek for the sun,
so in my dark hours I look for thee.

The sky is surrounded by dark clouds
and my heart by gloom, seeking after thy light, my
beloved sun.

When the sun is covered by clouds and darkness prevails,
then my heart cries aloud, "My sun, my beloved sun."

The dark clouds brought romance
between thee, my beloved, and me.

I shall penetrate the black heart
of the clouds to reach thee, my Lord.

Storm

My soul is still pointing to thee
though my life is going through a storm.

Thy invasion as through the storm
arouses my deepest passion for thee.

I hold ear to the depth of thy blessing
when the storm breaks through life's sea.

Fire

Fire, divine purifier,
purify my heart.

Fire, O power of God,
purify my mind from all evil.

Fire, in thee I see
the maker, purifier, and healer: God.

Let love's fire remain in my heart
and all else be burnt.

Let me live in thy warmth;
raise me above the coldness of the earth.

Kindle, Lord, fire in my heart,
that life may become clearer to me.

Let the tortures of life burn up all
*which keeps me from rising to thy spheres of freedom and
peace.*

Destroy, Lord, my infirmities
by the fire of thy love.

Raise my soul up
as the rising of the flame.

Let my false self be turned into ashes
that my true self be born as a phoenix.

Let the flame that rises in my heart
illuminate my path.

Sun

SUNSHINE:

Let the sun of thy glory
shine in my heart.

SUNRISE:

Raise my soul towards thee
with the rise of the sun.

SUNSET:

Let me unite with thee
at the sunset.

Let the sun of thy divine spirit rise from my heart,
that morn may break out of the darkness of life.

Wherever thy loving glance falleth,
a new sun riseth.

Beloved, the casting of thy glance causeth the sun to
rise
and with the turning of thy glance, the sun sets.

31

Since thy smile has created a new sun in my heart
I see the sun shine everywhere.

With the opening and the closing of thine eyes, beloved,
the sun rises and sets in my heart.

Moon

MOONLIGHT:

> Let my heart reflect thy light
> *as the moon reflects the sun.*

RISING MOON:

> Let my soul advance towards thee,
> *as the rising moon progresses towards fullness.*

WANING MOON:

> Let thy light be my torch
> *through the darkness of mind.*

> Let thy light guide my path
> *through the darkness of mind.*

FOR THE DAY OF THE FULL MOON:

> Fill my heart with thy light
> *so fully as the full moon.*

Let thy perfection be mine
and my imperfection be lost as the darkness in the full
moon.

Darkness of Night

Through the darkness of night
my soul seeks for thee.

Sky with Stars

Let my heart become a planet
in thy heaven.

Let me receive thy divine message
as the stars receive light from thy hidden face.

Fill my heart with thy love,
that my every teardrop may become a star.

Open a way through thy heavens,
that I may arrive at thy dwelling place.

Let my soul reflect thy light,
that every glance I cast may become a comet.

Air

Speak, God, to me
through the air.

Heal me, God,
by the waves of the air.

In the air I hear
thy consoling voice.

In the touch of the air
I feel thy sympathetic caress.

Lift my soul, air,
and carry it to his divine spheres.

The air moves my heart
to tears in thy love.

The air brings thy message
and turns me into ecstasy.

I rise above birth and death
through the waves of the air.

Air, carry the message of my feeling heart,
far and beyond.

Space

As invisible as space
(and as inconceivable as time)
is thy being, O Lord!

To RISE ABOVE WORRY AND FEAR:

Thou art present
all through space.

To SEEK THE TRUTH IN MYSTERY:

I behold through space
thy limitless presence.

Let me greet thee in space,
O formless and colorless God.

Fill my heart with thy beauty
as thou fillest with thy creation empty space.

Earth into earth, water into water,
let my soul immerse into thee through space.

Sky

Envelop me as in the light in thy divine spirit;
raise me from the denseness of the earth.

Wind

STRONG WIND:

> My soul blows towards thee
> *as the wind.*

GENTLE, SOFT WIND (THE WIND FLUTTERING IN LEAVES):

> Thou blowest my heart's fire
> *by fanning it with the fluttering leaves.*

> Every leaf becomes thy finger
> *when thou fillest the flute with thy breath.*

> Let me receive thy message
> *as the branches which swing in ecstasy.*

41

On Movement

I touch thy life in movement
and feel thy spirit in stillness.

Let thy every movement become a word for me,
which was lost for me so long.

Every movement of nature
is a signal from thee.

Every movement covereth
thy voice.

The whole universe is an instrument
whose rhythm is conducted by thy baton.

Let me see thy divine movement
in all moving things of the universe.

Let me see the secret
hidden behind thy movement.

42

Beings

Animals

I am sure that thou carest for me
as thou lookest after thy speechless creatures.

O shepherd of humanity,
thou lookest after all thy creatures.

Human Nature

In man I see, my beloved Lord,
thine own image.

I stand at thy gate
when I am in the presence of man.

When I greet man,
I bow at thy gate.

I find thy shrine
at the heart of man.

WOMAN (MEDITATIONS FOR MAN ON WOMAN):

I gently approach woman
lest I may disturb thy womanly tenderness.

Thy divine mercy is reflected
through the heart of the mother.

I recognize thy divine grace
in the tenderness of woman's heart.

In woman's virtue
I recognize thy divine purity.

I experience thy divine perfection
with woman, who completes my life.

Woman, my steppingstone
in the ascent towards thy shrine.

I experience thy perfection
in the union with my other half.

MAN (MEDITATIONS FOR WOMAN ON MAN):

In man I recognize
thy loving protection.

My soul's ideal is manifest to me
in the form of man.

In the arms of man I experience
thy divine embrace.

I experience thy divine perfection
with man, who completes my life.

Raise me above the denseness of life
and allow me to recognize man in thee.

Thou art the man,
all souls look to thee for love.

Childhood

I see thy divine purity
in the innocent face of the child.

Thy message I receive
through the happy smiles of the infant.

The air of heaven the child brings to me
when it comes on earth.

I depend entirely on thy protection, my Lord,
as an innocent child.

Guide me aright, my Lord;
I am as a child in thy divine path.

Purify my heart
as the heart of an innocent child.

Teach me innocence, O Lord,
through the child, an angel on earth.

I rise above all worries and bitterness of life
as a child.

Old Age

Let me approach near to thee
as I grow old.

In my veneration for the aged
I worship thee, O Lord.

In the grey hair of the aged
I see thy purity, O Lord.

The aged are my messengers
to thee, O Lord.

Bless me through the kind glance of the aged
and teach me in their words.

My soul is getting to be aged
and my heart is turning grey by thy silver light.

The Sage or Godly Man

To the godly man to whom all angels bow,
I bow.

Let thy servant, O Lord,
be my master.

My holy pilgrimage
is the sacred dwelling of the sage.

The presence of the godly man
for me is the holy river.

It is thou who comest on earth
to save humanity in the form of the sage.

Let my heart reflect
the spirit of the holy ones.

Let me enter thy dwelling
through the heart of thy holy one.

Let me become thy body,
Thou become my spirit, O holy one!

I lose my self in the self of the godly man
to unite with thee.

On the Prophet

Let me recognize thy visage
in the image of thy avatar.

Teach me, O Lord,
through the words of thy messenger.

Warn me, Lord, through thy prophet,
before I step into error.

Heal my soul
through the inspiring glance of thy messiah.

I see thy spirit, O Rasul,
under the veil of my spiritual guide.

Divinity I see
in thy spirit of Risalat.

Thine own ideal I see
in the perfection of Rasul.

My heart is no more mine,
it is thine own, my spiritual guide.

My soul is thy spirit, O Rasul;
now I exist no more.

I gave heart and soul to my guide, my teacher,
and what remains now is thine, O Lord.

On God

Thou knowest all my needs
and thou shalt grant them.

O knower of my heart,
fulfill my desires.

It is thou whom I see
in all names and forms.

Thou art closer to me
than myself.

Let thy might strengthen me,
(thy light inspire me),
and let thy love move my soul to the ultimate joy.

Make me conscious of thee,
that I may lose the consciousness of my being.

Let every movement of life
whisper thy name to my ears.

God, be thou before me when I am awake
and with me when I am asleep.

In thy nature
I feel thy presence.

O Creator,
who art hidden under thy wonderful creation.

Speak, God, to me
through thy nature.

I stand as a bridge
between thee and thy nature.

Lift, God, the curtain,
which divides thee from me.

Remove the wall from my sight
that I may attain thy presence.

Unveil thy face, O Lord,
that I may behold thy vision.

Let my self turn
into thy being.

Let my life become
thy soul.

Let me forget myself
in thy consciousness.

I drink the wine of thy presence
and lose myself in its intoxication.

One more cup, my beloved,
that I may entirely lose myself.

Let me be drowned in thy divine ocean
as a pearl in wine.

General

Let earth reflect heaven,
that I may read life as an open book.

Let thy word become
my life's expression.

Talk to me, my Lord;
the ears of my heart are listening.

Let my life be fruitful
in its every aspect.

Unfold thy secret through nature
and reveal thy mystery through my heart.

Let my mind bear sweet fruit and fragrant flowers,
as this tree is planted on the soil of thy spirit.

Every form I see is
thine own form, my Lord.

Every sound I hear is
thine own voice.

In fragrance I smell
the perfume of thy spirit.

In every word spoken to me,
I hear thy voice, my Lord.

All that touches me is
thine own touch.

In everything I taste
I experience the syrup of thy delicious spirit.

In every place
I recognize thee, my Lord.

Every word that touches my ears is
thy message.

Everything that touches me thrills me
with the joy of thy kiss.

Wherever I roam
I meet thee;
wherever I reach
I find thee, my Lord.

Wherever I look I see
thy glorying face;
whatever I touch
I touch thy beloved hand.

Whomever I see,
I see thee in his soul.

From whomever I take anything,
I take it from thee.

To whomever I give something,
I give it humbly to thee.

Whoever cometh to me,
to me it is thy call.

To whomever I call,
I call at thine own gate.

Whenever I nod to anyone,
I bow before thy throne.

In showing my sympathy to anyone,
I express my love to thee, my beloved.

On the Silence and Stillness
in Nature

Through the silence of nature,
I attain thy divine peace.

O sublime nature,
in thy stillness let my heart rest.

Thou art patiently awaiting the moment
to manifest through the silence of sublime nature.

O nature sublime, speak to me through silence,
for I am awaiting in silence, like you, the call of God.

O nature sublime,
through thy silence I hear thy cry.

My heart is tuned to the quietness
that the stillness of nature inspires.

O nature sublime, pregnant of divine spirit,
manifest as a prayer, which rises from my heart.

Speak, God, in silence,
*this moment my heart is in tune with the stillness of thy
nature.*

Though the ever-moving life is my nature,
thou art my very being, O stillness.

On Light and Shadow

All light is thy radiance,
and shade is the shadow of thy beauty.

Thou art in both: in light as radiance,
in the dark as shade.

Thou changest thy place,
but not thyself, O light.

Light is thy manifestation;
shade is thy withdrawing.

In the light thou art manifest;
in the shade thou art hidden.

Light is thine eye
and shade is its pupil.

The shade adds to the light
as zero adds to the figure.

Light represents thy heavens
and shade thy earth.

In the light I see thy beauty;
in shade I find thy mystery.

Light is thy face,
and shade is thy bosom.

On Colors

YELLOW:

> *In yellow I see*
> the flame of thy light.

> *I see in yellow*
> thy love and thy light.

> Thou hast adorned with yellow
> *the earth and thy heavens.*

> Let my heart ripen
> *as a green leaf ripens to yellow.*

> I see thy two wings
> *in the green water and the yellow earth.*

> Let the yellow flames of thy divine light
> *turn my false ego into ashes.*

SAFFRON:

> *In saffron shineth*
> the light of thy majesty.

Saffron is the color
of thy kingly grandeur.

In saffron I feel
thy passionate love.

Saffron brings
enchantment and heavenly joy to my heart.

BROWN:

In brown I watch
Thy soft smiles proving to me thy mild nature.

Thy ripe nature
manifests in brown.

In brown I see
thy constant endurance.

Thy charity of heart
manifests in the color brown.

GOLD:

O alchemist eternal,
turn my heart into gold.

67

Orange:

In orange I see
thy light culminated, perfected.

The sun brings to me
thy greetings, clad in an orange garb.

I see in orange
the glorious vision of thy heavenly riches.

Through orange thou bringest delight
to my yearning heart.

In orange I see
thy wisdom and thy compassion.

Red:

In the red color I see
thy glowing countenance.

In red I see
the bleeding of thy heart in sympathy for thy
creatures.

Red shows me
thy life in its perfect glow.

Red brings life
to my hungry heart.

Dye my heart red,
that it may take the color of thine own life.

VIOLET:

O ever-youthful beloved, from violet I hear
thy silent groan of heart.

Beloved, I hear thy soft lamentation
in violet.

PURPLE:

In purple I find
thy deepest woes.

I sympathize with thy grief,
seeing it manifest in purple

SCARLET:

Thy deep sorrow spearest through my heart,
rising through the scarlet blood.

Scarlet brings to my heart
thy eternal martyrdom.

PINK:

The color pink raises in my heart
love for thy being.

BLUE:

In the blue color I get
the glimpse of thy heavens.

I see heaven shining out
in thy blue eyes.

I behold the blue of thine eyes
in the sky.

Out of blue comes thy uplifting influence,
which raiseth me from earth.

In blue I see
the purity of thy nature.

Raise me high
in the blue spheres of thy heaven.

I feel thy presence most
when all is blue to me.

Green:

In the green color I see
thy life springing.

I see thy two wings
in the green water and the yellow earth.

The green carpet of thy heaven
is spread on the earth.

Reflect, God, thy compassion
in the tone of the green nature.

Thy heart's emotions
are expressed in the ever-rising waves of the green sea.

71

Through green thou speakest;
through blue thou art silent.

Let my soul move in thy thought
as the green in the forest.

Give me the patience of the green trees
that stand still, awaiting thy command.

I ask for the bowl of green poison
that bringeth the life that follows death.

WHITE:

In white I see thy purity
manifested to my eyes.

In white lilies I bring thee
an offering of my open heart.

BLACK:

In the color black
I feel the depth of thy being.

Thou showest in black
thy eternal being.

72

In black thou givest me a proof
of being above all changes.

Who is behind utter darkness:
thy endless self.

Black is death,
yet life eternal.

GREY:

I recognize thy face
covered under the grey veil.

In grey I see the sign
of the maturity of thy spirit.

In the heart of grey
the world is reflected.

Thy heavens are supported
by grey ceilings.

My deep sigh rises as a grey vapor
for thy consoling words as rain.

On Straight Lines

In the straight line
thou art still.

The straight line tells me
thou art the only being.

The straight line speaks
of thy justice.

The straight line shows me
the path to thee.

The straight line expresses
the beginning of creation.

The straight line tells us
that thou art one alone.

The straight line cries aloud
that there is none besides thee.

The straight line promises
his ease.

The straight line represents
clearness.

Different Movements

Inward movement means strength and control.

Outward movement means exhaustion and expulsion.

Zigzag movement means strength but destruction.

Side movement directed from right to left means strength and power.

Side movement directed from left to right means gentleness and modesty.

Side movement directed upwards means love and purity.

Side movement directed downwards means affection and humility.

On Horizontal Lines

The horizontal line expresses the hindrance on the path.

The horizontal line conveys death.

The horizontal line suggests stillness.

The horizontal line is the obstacle.

The horizontal line is preventive of action.

The horizontal line is the sign of destruction.

The horizontal line shows annihilation.

The horizontal line is expressive of mortality.

The horizontal line is a sign of failure.

The Cross

The horizontal line with the vertical is the sign of perfection.

The horizontal line with the vertical is the sign of life.

The horizontal line with the vertical is the sign of perfect joy.

The horizontal line with the vertical is the sign of experience.

The horizontal line with the vertical is the cause of resurrection.

The horizontal line with the vertical is the means of divine perfection.

The Circle

The circle is the sign of God.

The circle is the sign of perfection.

The circle is the sign of unchangeableness.

The circle is the sign of the beginning of life and of the extinction of life.

The circle is the sign of beginning and of ending.

The circle is the sign of the source and of the goal.

The circle means nothing, everything, and all things.

The circle is life and is death.

The circle is richness.

The circle is an unending pain and an everlasting joy.

The circle is the lake in which the souls are lost and the fountain where the souls arise.

The circle expresses the whirlwind through all the aspects of life.

The circle represents the world.

The circle represents the planets.

The circle represents the secret.

The circle represents the opening and the closing.

The circle represents the absorption and the expulsion.

What Color Flowers One Should Give

One should use:

For a dying person, white flowers, with the thought that his passing should be peaceful.

For disorders of the blood, white flowers, preferably jasmine.

For nervous young people of an emotional nature who have not found themselves, white lilies.

For nervous persons unstable in mind and body, yellow flowers. Tulips are best, but all kinds of yellow flowers are good.

For anemia, red tulips, red roses, red flowers of any kind.

For a person who fears death, who is restless and in despair on his sickbed, pink roses or pink flowers.

For persons who are so strongly impressed by illness that they can't get better, blue flowers.

For obsessed persons or those who are ill from some evil spirit's influence, any kind of orchid.

(Always remember the thought behind the flower.)

What Different Flowers Give

The rose gives development.

The orchid gives artistry.

White flowers give development of character.

Flowers with perfume give personality.

Yellow flowers give brilliance.

Sapphire flowers give joy.

Purple flowers give weight to the personality.

Stones

Emerald = progress, productivity, especially in beauty and art.

Sapphire = art and inspiration.

Ruby = love, sorrow, and difficulties.

Topaz = harmony.

Diamond = righteousness.

Never use a pearl. It stands for imprisonment because it comes out of a shell. It brings confinement and wealth, with all the sorrows which belong to it.

Do not wear an opal. It has all colors; it represents positive and negative, and that is not good. There must be either one or the other. They are both good, but not at the same time.

Use of Colors

Healing colors are light colors:
White, cream, spring green, sky blue, flower yellow.

For skin disease:
White, cream.

For nervous illness and consumption:
Sky blue.

For nervous illness:
Flower yellow.

For worn-out, depleted, and old people:
Spring green.

For crippled people:
Sandalwood color (yellow-brown earth).

For orphans:
Spring green, yellow, pink, sky blue.

For the blind:
Sky blue.

For the insane:
Sandalwood color.

For cremation halls:
Smoke color, from grey to white going upwards.
    (Never use mauve for this occasion. It is the color
    of mourning and is bad for the dead. A person who
    is expecting danger or sorrow has a mauve aura.)

For students' buildings:
Dark amber and red, with an amber light for inspiration,
    youth, imagination, intellectual studies.

For prisons:
Blue of all shades.

For business places:
Deep, striking colors; blue, pink.

For churches and devotion:
Red, pink, blue, green, yellow, silver, gold.

For the higher aspect (illumination):
Yellow.

For the religious emotion (faith):
Red.

For aspiration:
Blue.

For spreading a religious message:
Green.

For virtue (piety):
Silver.

For grace and benediction:
Gold.

For clothing:
In daily life do not wear purple, especially not purple in
which red dominates, for it brings destruction. For
mysticism and spiritual purposes purple is good,
but not for daily life.
Do not wear red and blue in combination. This
brings thunder, and when fire is in the air it brings
destruction.

For convents (nuns):
Mauve (*not* scarlet).

For monasteries (monks):
Pink, cream.

For virgin girls:
Turquoise.

For future brides:
Coral red.

For consoling:
Spring green, yellow.

To calm down:
The least striking colors, yellowish brown. Mountains,
    thickly covered with green, deep valleys.

Against melancholy:
Apricot. The more sky, stars, sun, moon, the better.

To get above lower thoughts:
Cream. Angels, churches, domes.

INAYAT KHAN BIOGRAPHICAL NOTE

Pir-o-Murshid Inayat Khan (1882-1927), founder of the Sufi Order International, came to the West as a representative of the highest musical traditions of his native India. He brought with him a message of love, harmony, and beauty that was both the quintessence of Sufi teaching and a revolutionary approach to the harmonizing of Western and Eastern spirituality.

Inayat Khan dedicated his early life to the mastery of the subtle intricacies of classical Indian music, winning the high title of *Tansen* from the Nizam of

Hyderabad, a powerful ruler and renowned patron of the musical arts.

In the fulfillment of his quest for a spiritual teacher, Inayat Khan took initiation from Shaykh al-Mashaykh Sayed Muhammed Abu Hashim Madani. While Madani was an initiator of the four main Sufi lineages in India, his primary connection was with the Chishti Order. At the end of Inayat Khan's apprenticeship, his teacher enjoined him to travel to the West and harmonize the spiritualities of East and West.

On September 13 of 1910 Inayat Khan began an odyssey that would encompass three continents and transform the lives of thousands. He eventually settled in Suresnes, a suburb of Paris. During his sixteen years in the West, he created a school of spiritual training based upon the traditional teachings of the Chishti Sufis and infused with a revolutionary vision—a vision of the unity of religious ideals and the awakening of humanity to the divinity within.